My Happy Goldfinch

By

Christina Rioux

with illustrations by Natalia Mercedes Padró

FCP

Full Court Press
Englewood Cliffs, New Jersey

Published in the United States of America
by Full Court Press, 601 Palisade Avenue
Englewood Cliffs, NJ 07632
fullcourtpressnj.com

ISBN 978-1-938812-69-9

Book design by Barry Sheinkopf for Bookshapers.Com
(www.bookshapers.com)

Illustrations by Natalia Mercedes Padró

Author photo by Derek Fiore

Colophon by Liz Sedlack

A portion of the proceeds of this book will be donated
to the Arthritis Foundation

To my mother,

MARTHA ELLEN BARTH

who showed me that love, no matter in what form—
a cool breeze on your face, a delicious smell,
a familiar song, a snowflake, or a yellow bird—
will always find a way to warm your heart.

As Momma was lying quite sick in her bed,

she said not to worry inside my sweet head—

for "Whenever a goldfinch you happen to see,

be friendly, be happy. . .for it will be me!"

So I searched and I looked over each branch and tree,

yet never a goldfinch did I ever see.

I never knew looking for a bird could be so much fun,

especially if I could find me a bright yellow one.

Then once on the Palisades, down by the River,

I heard a bright song that at once made me quiver—

a goldfinch's song (I could tell from the sound).

My Momma was calling—in the bird, she'd been found!

From the edge of my eye I just managed to spy

a burst of bright yellow like a roller coaster in the sky.

I jumped up and down, thrilled and elated

at finding the place where my love could be stated.

So I went to the bird store and asked Mr. Pete,

"What do the goldfinches most like to eat?"

"Why, thistle for whistle, and seed for their speed.

If you give 'em those two, they'll be happy indeed."

I bought them right then, and a little blue tray,

then hiked up to a forest rock, and set it to stay.

I filled the tray with seeds, slipped away in a dash

and waited for the goldfinch to find all that stash.

A few days went by till I came back to see

that the goldfinch had fed and was singing with glee!

And, looking round, my eyes grew very wide,

for what I saw next made me so warm inside:

There in the honeysuckle, calm and at rest,

was a momma goldfinch sitting on her cute little nest!

She'd started a family with her handsome mate.

They'd spend years in a spot that *I'd* helped create!

Then I looked up and saw a big "X" in the sky
where two crossing planes had left paths way up high.

I knew what it meant, as my heart filled with love—

It was a KISS sent by Momma from Heaven above.

So keep in your heart all the people you love

because someday they'll come back to see you. . .

as a goldfinch, a cardinal—or maybe a dove.

www.Ingramcontent.com/pod-product-compliance
Lightning Source LLC
Chambersburg PA
CBHW040852100426

42813CB00015B/2779